DATE DUE

DEMCO 38-297

Susan B. Anthony

JUNIOR ■ WORLD ■ BIOGRAPHIES

Susan B. Anthony

PAMELA LEVIN

CHELSEA JUNIORS

a division of CHELSEA HOUSE PUBLISHERS

CHELSEA HOUSE PUBLISHERS

Editorial Director Richard Rennert
Executive Managing Editor Karyn Gullen Browne
Executive Editor Sean Dolan
Copy Chief Robin James
Picture Editor Adrian G. Allen
Manufacturing Director Gerald Levine
Systems Manager Lindsey Ottman
Production Coordinator Marie Claire Cebrián-Ume

JUNIOR WORLD BIOGRAPHIES

Senior Editor Kathy Kuhtz

Staff for SUSAN B. ANTHONY
Associate Editor Martin Schwabacher
Copy Editor Philip Koslow
Editorial Assistants Robert Kimball Green, Mary B. Sisson
Senior Designer Marjorie Zaum
Picture Researcher Sandy Jones

First Printing

1 3 5 7 9 8 6 4 2

Library of Congress Cataloging-in-Publication Data
Levin, Pamela.
    Susan B. Anthony/ Pamela Levin.
      p. cm.—(Junior world biographies)
    Includes bibliographical references and index.
ISBN 0-7910-1762-1
      0-7910-1965-9 (pbk.)
1. Anthony, Susan B. (Susan Brownell)—Juvenile literature. 2. Feminists—
United States—Biography—Juvenile literature. 3. Suffragette—United
States—Biography—Juvenile literature. I. Title. II. Series.
HQ1413.A55L48 1993   92-31428
305.4'2'092—dc20   CIP
[B]   AC

Contents

Susan B. Anthony was 52 years old when she was arrested for voting in 1872.

1
"We, the People"

In 1872, a curious crowd in Canandaigua, New York, awaited Susan Brownell Anthony, who was to deliver a speech. When Anthony arrived, she began to address the crowd:

> Friends and fellow-citizens, I stand before you under indictment [officially charged] for the alleged crime of having voted at the last presidential election, without having a lawful right to vote. . . . I not only committed no crime, but instead simply exercised my citizen's right.

In 1872, women still did not have the legal right to vote in the United States. Susan B. Anthony had often spoken of her belief in equal rights for women. But her decision to register to vote that year took the country by surprise—particularly the Rochester election officials who had seen her marching up the street toward them. On the morning of November 1, Anthony had persuaded her older sister, Guelma, and her younger sisters, Hannah and Mary, to join her in her march downtown. With them came 12 other Rochester women who had been persuaded by Anthony's stirring pleas to add their own names to the voter lists at the local barbershop where registration took place.

Anthony had read to the marchers an advertisement that she had seen in the newspaper that morning:

> Citizens, register now! If you were not permitted the right to vote, you would fight for the right, undergo all privations for it, face death for it. You have it now at the cost of five minutes'

time to be spent in seeking your place of registration, and having your name entered.

It struck Anthony that the newspaper ad had stated nothing about registration being for men only. In fact, it said "citizens," a term used in the Constitution to refer to the people of the United States. But the election inspector laughed at the women who wanted to sign up to vote and said that they should go home to their children. Anthony became angry. She read to him from the Fourteenth and Fifteenth amendments to the Constitution. These amendments had been created to assert and protect the rights of the newly freed slaves. Susan B. Anthony and her friends understood the meaning of the words to include women as well:

Fourteenth Amendment:

All persons born or naturalized in the United States . . . are citizens of the United States.

Fifteenth Amendment:

The right of citizens of the United States to vote shall not be denied or abridged . . . on account of race, color, or previous condition of servitude [slavery].

Because the women threatened to stay in the barbershop until their names were written down, the inspector agreed to register them. Four days later, on November 5, many of these women cast their ballots for one of the candidates for the office of president. That day, Anthony wrote to her good friend and fellow activist Elizabeth Cady Stanton,

Following Anthony's example, these women attempted to vote in 1875 in New York City, but they were turned away by election officials.

"Well, I have been and gone and done it, positively voted this morning at 7 o'clock."

To be able to vote was an important liberty for women. Without suffrage, or the right to vote, women's opinions would not mean anything in matters concerning the state or federal governments. It was only recently that the law had been changed to allow women to own property. Their clothes, even their children, had been considered the property of their husbands. Women could only work in certain jobs, and they usually received much lower pay than men doing the same work. They were not even particularly encouraged to

speak in public, although pioneering women, such as Anthony, were trying to change that.

Although casting her vote created a great moment in women's history, Anthony understood that there would be consequences. On Thanksgiving Day, 1872, U.S. deputy marshal E. J. Keeney came to Anthony's home and hesitantly told Anthony that she was under arrest. It was his job to bring her to the office of the U.S. commissioner of elections in Rochester. But, he hastily explained to the dignified silver-haired woman, she could go alone whenever she was ready.

Anthony said she would not think of going by herself, and dramatically extended her arms for handcuffs. Ignoring the invitation, the flustered marshal escorted his prisoner out of the house and down to the corner, where he helped her board a streetcar. When the conductor asked for her fare, her response could be heard at the back of the car. "I'm traveling at the expense of the government," she said. "This gentleman is escorting me to jail.

Ask him for my fare." Keeney reluctantly agreed to buy her ticket.

Anthony's pretrial hearing was held in a small courtroom that had once been used for trials of runaway slaves. During the hearing, the elections commissioner asked Anthony if she had any doubt of her right to vote. "Not a particle," she replied.

Anthony was not put in jail but was released on bail. During the winter months before her trial, she traveled long hours by train and horse carriage to publicize her cause. She toured city after city, lecturing, attending town meetings, and calling assemblies of her own. In New York, in only 30 days, she spoke in all 29 villages of her home county of Monroe.

Anthony's fiery speeches won her so much sympathy that two weeks before her trial the case was moved to Ontario County. Anthony and her supporters flooded that county as well with passionate appeals for justice. Anthony spoke on the topic, "Is It a Crime for a United States Citizen To Vote?" A supporter's speech was titled, "The United States on Trial, Not Susan B. Anthony."

The people to whom Anthony spoke in Canandaigua, New York, had special importance to her. This town had been chosen as the location of her trial instead of Rochester, where Anthony had many friends and much political influence. For her listeners in Canandaigua, she had a special

In 1873, Anthony was declared guilty of the crime of voting illegally, simply because she was a woman.

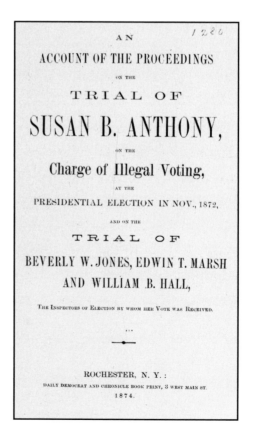

AN
ACCOUNT OF THE PROCEEDINGS
ON THE
TRIAL OF
SUSAN B. ANTHONY,
ON THE
Charge of Illegal Voting,
AT THE
PRESIDENTIAL ELECTION IN NOV., 1872,
AND ON THE
TRIAL OF
BEVERLY W. JONES, EDWIN T. MARSH
AND WILLIAM B. HALL,
THE INSPECTORS OF ELECTION BY WHOM HER VOTE WAS RECEIVED.

...

ROCHESTER, N. Y. :
DAILY DEMOCRAT AND CHRONICLE BOOK PRINT, 3 WEST MAIN ST.
1874.

message: "There is and can be but one safe principle of government—equal rights to all."

Anthony then reminded her audience of the words in the U.S. Constitution: "It was we, the people, not we, the white male citizens, nor we, the male citizens; but we, the whole people who formed this Union." She wanted to make sure the people around her knew her views, for she was going to be in court the following day.

On June 17, 1873, Judge Ward Hunt announced: "Susan B. Anthony, you are brought to trial for voting unlawfully." Judge Hunt vigorously opposed Anthony's feminist beliefs. He refused to allow Anthony to speak, saying women were not competent to be witnesses in court. Then, despite her lawyer's protests, the judge immediately proclaimed Anthony guilty of the charges. He not only ordered the jury to pronounce a guilty verdict, but he then dismissed its members before they even had a moment to open their mouths. In silence, Susan B. Anthony glared at the judge who had not given her a fair trial. Henry Selden,

Anthony's lawyer, complained loudly, but Judge Hunt was ready to read his sentence.

"Has the prisoner anything to say why sentence should not be pronounced?" he asked. This was not the question to ask a woman who had been speaking nonstop for several months about why her arrest was unjust. She jumped to her feet to respond to him.

"Your honor," she said, "I have many things to say. You have trampled underfoot every principle of our government. My natural rights, my civil rights, my political rights, my judicial rights, are all alike ignored."

The judge ordered her to sit down and be silent, but Anthony kept on talking. "The prisoner," he insisted, "has been tried according to established forms of law."

"Yes, your honor," Anthony shot back, "but by forms of law all made by men, interpreted by men, administered by men, and against women."

By now the judge was shouting. "The court orders the prisoner to sit down," he thundered. "It will not allow another word!" When Anthony halted at last, Hunt delivered her sentence: a fine of $100 plus court costs.

Anthony responded in a controlled voice. "May it please your honor," she said, "I shall never pay a dollar of your unjust penalty." She never did. Because Judge Hunt knew that if he imprisoned her she could appeal her case to the U.S. Supreme Court (and possibly win), he released her. His actions, wrote a furious Anthony, were "the greatest outrage history ever witnessed."

But in the long run, victory would be hers. Exactly 100 years after Anthony's birth, women finally won the right to vote. The Nineteenth Amendment to the U.S. Constitution, adopted in 1920, became known as the Susan B. Anthony Amendment.

At age 28, Anthony was the headmistress of the "female department" of Canajoharie Academy. She had recently begun wearing brightly colored dresses in a striking departure from the Quakers' severe dress code.

2
Growing Up

Susan B. Anthony was born on February 15, 1820, near Adams, a little town surrounded by hills in western Massachusetts. At that time, her parents, Daniel Anthony and Lucy Read Anthony, were living with her two-year-old sister, Guelma, on a small farm. On either side were the farms of her grandparents. There were other families nearby, and on Sundays they would gather at the Adams meetinghouse for silent prayer.

Susan's family belonged to the Quaker church, also known as the Society of Friends. The

Quakers preached simple living and "brotherly love," encouraging education and hard work for all their members, male or female. Because of her father's deep belief in Quaker ways, Susan had some opportunities that many young women did not have. The Anthony children all learned to read when they were very young—Susan's grandmother taught her to read when she was four. When they were ready, they all walked up the hill to the schoolhouse that their Grandfather Anthony had built.

This square wooden building was the same one where Lucy Read had sat learning her lessons years before, taught by Daniel Anthony. When 23-year-old Lucy and 26-year-old Daniel fell in love and married in 1817, they created great concern in the Adams community: the new Mrs. Anthony had not been raised as a Quaker. Although she had grown up next door, her world of colorful clothes, singing, dancing, and parties was very different from that of the "plain" Anthonys. Marriage outside the Quaker faith was normally prohibited by Quakers, and when Lucy and Daniel wed, Lucy had to promise to give up her life-style and adopt her husband's.

Lucy Anthony had been used to having fun, and the work of raising seven children and looking after the visitors who frequently stayed at the house exhausted her. The Anthony family grew quickly: Guelma was born in 1818, Susan in 1820, Hannah in 1821, and Daniel in 1824. Three more children—Mary, Eliza, and Merritt—would be born after the family moved to New York in 1826. Lucy Anthony had promised her husband that she would not sing to her children because it was forbidden by the Quakers, but her warm, loving spirit came through in her gentle care. Susan later wrote about her mother, recalling "dear mother, toiling unremittingly through the long day." She carried this impression of her mother burdened by work throughout her own life.

Daniel Anthony greatly influenced Susan's life through his opinions and his actions. The Quakers believed very strongly in education, and

Daniel Anthony wanted his children to learn as much as possible at school. This was unusual in the early 1800s. Although most children went to school, many did not continue after they reached the age of 12. Boys were often expected to work, helping on the family farm or business, and many girls never went to school at all. Girls were expected to learn how to raise families and how to handle household chores, such as cooking and sewing.

Daniel Anthony, following Quaker practice, chose to treat his children as equals. The girls

Daniel and Lucy Read Anthony, Susan's parents, encouraged Susan in her battles for women's rights, temperance, and the abolition of slavery.

attended school, and then they prepared to earn their living as teachers (even though they *might* marry some day). Daniel Anthony also encouraged all his children to speak up and express their own opinions. No "proper" Quaker children, however, learned music, put on plays, drew pictures, or played with toys or games. In school or at home, Quakers considered these activities unsuitable.

One Quaker belief that Susan's father instilled in his children was his opposition to alcohol. Women at the time had no protection from drunken husbands who beat them. A woman did not have the legal right to divorce a man even if he was drunken, abusive, and failed to support his family. Thousands of people concerned about the problem of alcohol abuse flocked to the *temperance movement*, which opposed the consumption of alcohol.

Susan's father was a firm advocate of temperance. In those days, most businessmen offered their customers a drink of rum after a sale.

Daniel Anthony impressed his daughter by refusing to serve alcohol to his customers. Later, Susan herself would become a leader in the temperance movement.

Quakers also believed in equality between people of all races. Daniel Anthony strongly opposed slavery and refused to use cotton produced by slave labor in his mill, which made cotton cloth. One day a stranger came to the Anthonys' house. Sitting at the kitchen table in the candlelight, he talked with Susan's father long into the night. Six-year-old Susan and her sisters whispered to each other about what the visit could mean.

The stranger, Judge McLean, had asked Daniel Anthony to manage a mill the judge owned in Battenville, New York. Anthony had wanted to expand his operation, and now Judge McLean had offered him a large mill to run and financial support. He wasted no time in moving his family by horse-drawn wagon the 40 miles to Battenville.

Susan, Guelma, and Hannah began attending Battenville's one-room schoolhouse. One evening, while at the supper table, Susan announced to her family that she was learning long division in class. But, she said, she could not always hear the lesson, because the teacher taught division only to the boys, who sat at the front of the room. When Susan asked to hear the explanations too, the teacher had told her "not to worry your pretty little head about such things."

Although it was common for girls to be excluded from such lessons, when Daniel Anthony saw Susan's interest he decided to build his own school alongside the Anthonys' new house, where girls and boys could learn as equals. Later, he started an evening school for his mill workers to attend after their day's labor. "Half the employees of the factory were there, learning to read and write or spell," Susan recalled. "Father would do the teaching himself. . . . He regarded his employees as his family." The Anthony house was always full of people. The schoolteachers and several girls who worked at the mill ate and slept there. As soon as Lucy Anthony had cooked and cleaned up one meal, it was time to begin work on the next. Before Eliza was born, Mrs. Anthony became too ill to work at all. For several months Guelma, Susan, and Hannah, ages 14, 12, and 10, did all the cooking and housework for the large group of boarders, which also included a dozen bricklayers who were working on the house.

Susan watched enviously as the mill girls went off to their jobs each morning. She liked the idea of earning money for work. Most of the mill girls received $1.50 per week, and many sent their wages home to help their families. Susan could only dream about working at the mill while she helped her sisters knead and bake 20 loaves of bread each day. Soon, though, after Lucy Anthony was well enough to be in charge again, Susan had her chance to go to the mill.

A spooler who became sick had to be replaced for two whole weeks. For Susan, it was an opportunity to explore her father's mill and to meet the many girls and women who worked in the large, noisy rooms. She quickly learned to

A popular 19th-century temperance poster warns of the dangers posed by drinking alcohol.

position the spools on the huge machines that spun brightly colored cotton thread. Day after day, Susan did the same job, watching the twirling thread, and she was delighted when she could take her pay home. She spent her money on a set of china for her mother. Susan decided that she liked working on her own, even if it meant doing hard work or working long hours.

Susan also learned her first lesson on women's rights in the mill. A woman named Sally Ann Hyatt knew how to fix the machinery better than anyone else. But when it came to choosing a supervisor, Susan's father selected a man. "Since Sally Ann knows much more about weaving and the machinery than he does," Susan asked, "why didn't you appoint her supervisor instead?" She was shocked when her father answered, "Super-vision of labor has always been for men, Susan."

Susan was 16 when she got her first real job, as a private tutor for a family in nearby Easton. She taught the children to read and write, living with them through the winter months. She had already spent the two previous summers working as a teacher's assistant in the Battenville school, but in Easton she taught on her own.

Even though she had begun to work, her father still encouraged her to continue her education. Because there were no suitable schools nearby, in 1837 she enrolled at Deborah Moulson's Select Female Seminary, a Quaker school for girls in Philadelphia, Pennsylvania. Guelma had begun taking classes there a year earlier. Susan, escorted by her father, spent nearly a week traveling the 300 miles to reach the seminary.

Far from home for the first time in her life, Susan became homesick and depressed, despite being surrounded by other girls her own age. She was not simply lonely. The school headmistress was a stern woman who constantly found fault with her students. According to the entries Susan wrote in her diary, Miss Moulson expected an impossible perfection in behavior and schoolwork. Although she tried to improve herself with great determination, Susan felt that she always did poorly. "I think so much of my resolutions to do better," she wrote, "that even my dreams are filled with these desires."

Once Susan even received a harsh lecture because Miss Moulson did not like the way she dotted her *i*'s. "This was like an Electrical shock to me," Susan wrote in her diary. "I rushed upstairs to my room where, without restraint, I could give vent to my tears."

Susan had been at the seminary for a year, and Guelma for two years, when their father asked them to return home. All over the United States, an economic depression was creating hard times for families, and the Anthonys were no exception. Daniel Anthony's mill went bankrupt, and everything he owned would have to be sold to pay his debts. As a result, he could not continue to pay tuition for his daughters' schooling. Even the bright house with the memorable schoolroom had to be sold, along with most of the family's possessions, including Lucy Anthony's wedding mementos and the girls' best dresses.

Susan never forgot how unfair she thought it was that her mother had to give up everything she owned to pay her husband's business debts. But legally, everything that belonged to her was her *husband's* property. Susan was able to buy back a few of her parents' most prized possessions with money she had saved from her small teacher's salary. But the episode provided a further lesson in the need for women's rights.

After selling their house, the family moved to the nearby village of Hardscrabble, New York, later called Center Falls. Susan helped out as much as she could; she described her efforts in her diary: "Spent today at the spinning wheel. . . . Baked 21 loaves of bread. . . . Have been weaving for several days." Deciding she could help her family more by bringing in a salary, she left for another teaching job, this time in New Rochelle, New York.

The Quakers in New Rochelle also supported equality for blacks—but not all of them practiced what they preached. "The Friends raised quite a fuss about a colored man sitting in the meeting-house, and some left on account of it," Anthony wrote in her diary in disgust. "What a lack of Christianity is this!" Anthony was further appalled when three "educated and refined" young black women were told they had to sit in the balcony. Anthony tried to make up for the rude treatment the visitors received; afterward in a letter to a friend she described her pleasure in "drinking tea with them. They are indeed fine *ladies.*"

In 1840, she returned to Center Falls for her sister Guelma's wedding. Susan took a job in the local school to be near her family. Although the male teacher she replaced had been paid $10 per week, Susan's salary was only $2.50. Once again, she had been discriminated against because she was a woman.

Anthony's opinion of men was not raised by the behavior of her cousin Margaret's husband. Once when Margaret lay desperately ill after the birth of her fourth child, her husband complained of a headache. When the sick woman said that she had one, too, her husband replied, "Oh, mine is the real headache, genuine pain, yours is a sort of natural consequence." A few weeks later, Margaret was dead. Anthony would never forget the man's disrespect and heartlessness.

Over the next few years, several young men would ask Susan to marry them, but she was not impressed by any of them. One, for example, she described as a "real soft-headed old bachelor." In any case, she had no desire to devote the rest of her life to housework. After the marriage of a friend to a man of whom Susan had a low opinion, she wrote in her diary, "Tis passing strange that a girl possessed of common sense should be willing to marry a lunatic—but so it is."

*Elizabeth Cady Stanton, shown here with
two of her six children, split her time between
working with Anthony for women's rights and caring
for her large family.*

3

To Fight
for a Cause

In 1846, Anthony accepted her most important job yet: headmistress of the "female department" at Canajoharie Academy, a well-known school in upstate New York. For the next three years she so impressed the residents with her brilliant leadership that one called her "the smartest woman ever to come to Canajoharie."

Living for the first time in a non-Quaker household, Anthony shed some of her Quaker ways. She started wearing colorful, stylish clothes and learned to dance, which she enjoyed immensely. She even attended a circus.

Anthony was pleased to be earning her own salary, unlike married women. When her sisters teased her by calling her "an old maid," she teased back, comparing herself to her newlywed sister, Hannah, who could no longer work and buy her own dresses. Susan wrote, "I suppose she feels rather sad that she is married and can no longer have nice clothes."

Shattered by the death of her cousin Margaret, however, Susan returned home to be with her family, who now lived in Rochester. The Anthony farm had become a place where people gathered to discuss the abolition of slavery. Among the frequent guests were Frederick Douglass, a former slave who was a national leader in the fight against slavery, and William Lloyd Garrison, the publisher of an abolitionist newspaper. Susan was quickly drawn into the political discussions, and she became a passionate abolitionist.

Anthony's first public speech was not about slavery, however, but about temperance. After joining the Daughters of Temperance in Canajoharie—women were not allowed in the main group, the Sons of Temperance—she became an energetic leader for the Rochester chapter. She rushed from event to event, organizing festivals and suppers to raise money for the popular cause. Anthony was so successful in her efforts that she soon became the society's traveling representative to temperance conventions held in other cities.

It was at one of these conferences that she met Amelia Bloomer, a feminist who published a temperance newspaper "devoted to the interests of women." Bloomer's name later became known for the baggy pants, called "bloomers," that some women wore under loose, comfortable skirts to replace the tight corsets and stiff, hooped skirts that made their household labors doubly difficult.

Bloomer introduced Anthony to Elizabeth Cady Stanton, who had organized the first women's rights convention in 1848 in Seneca

Falls, New York. "I like her thoroughly," Stanton had said of Anthony, and the two quickly became fast friends.

One meeting that both Anthony and Stanton attended finally made Anthony focus specifically on women's rights. In 1852, the Sons of Temperance held a convention in Albany, New York. Anthony listened to the discussions for a long time. Upon rising to express her own opinions, however, she was told that "the sisters were not invited here to speak but to listen and learn." Had the "sisters" worked all year long only to sit quietly? Susan B. Anthony stormed angrily out of the meeting hall.

Joining her later that evening in a cold, smoke-filled church basement, a handful of other strong-minded women helped her to form a new, independent group. The Woman's State Temperance Society, as the new organization was called, would hold its own convention. Anthony led the organization of the conference. It became the first of many joint projects that she and Elizabeth Cady Stanton coordinated. Stanton, dressed in the radical bloomer costume, was elected president of the new society. She surprised even the most radical women by suggesting that drunkenness could be reason for divorce. Anthony was impressed by both her courage and eloquence.

Throughout the following year, Anthony toured the state of New York to speak in crowded auditoriums on the "evils of alcohol." Stanton, home with her children, sent encouraging letters, and Anthony responded with reports on her experiences.

Gradually, Anthony came to believe that women must have the right to vote before they could really change anything. By the time the second annual Woman's State Temperance Convention was held in 1853, Anthony completely agreed with Stanton on this issue. In her opening address, Stanton said, "We have been obliged to preach Woman's Rights because many, instead of listening to what we had to say on Temperance, have questioned the right of women to speak on any subject."

Unfortunately, the men whom they had allowed to join the organization had grown in number, and the men not only disagreed with Stanton and Anthony but took control of the whole society. Having formed the group just so they would not be dominated by men, the two women resigned in protest from the organization they had created. But the two friends were now a determined and powerful force for women's rights.

Anthony and Stanton decided to approach New York State lawmakers to demand legal property rights for married women. Reaching their goal was going to be difficult, because all of the legislators were men. They had little interest in working for women's equality. Anthony, remembering how her mother's possessions were auctioned 15 years earlier, was ready to do whatever was necessary to win. "Woman must have a purse of her own," she wrote in her diary, "and how can this be, so long as the law denies to the wife all right to both the individual and joint earnings? There is no true freedom for woman without the possession of equal property rights, and these can be obtained only through legislation."

Stanton and Anthony devised a plan of action. Stanton, an experienced writer and a powerful speaker, would present their arguments at the next state legislative assembly. Anthony, rounding up a team of volunteers throughout the state, began collecting signatures on petitions proposing new property laws.

Tramping through snow and ice as they went from one home to the next, the women met many people who disagreed with them. Their hard work paid off, however. Six thousand people were willing to sign their names in favor of equal property rights, and 4,000 more supported woman suffrage (voting rights for women).

In February 1854, Elizabeth Cady Stanton addressed the lawmakers. She spoke persuasively on property rights, wages, children, and the need for women to be recognized as citizens by the law. "It is folly," she told them, "to talk of a mother moulding the character of her son, when all

Anthony's demands for equality met with many hostile responses, including this cartoon entitled "The Woman Who Dared," which appeared after she was arrested for voting.

mankind, backed up by law and public sentiment, conspire to destroy her influence. But when one woman's moral power shall speak through the ballot-box, then shall her influence be seen and felt." She also, for the first time, proposed women's suffrage. As Stanton finished speaking, Anthony presented the petitions with 10,000 signatures. She also made sure that each legislator had a copy of Stanton's speech.

It was too soon for laws to change, though. The men quickly dismissed Stanton and Anthony's proposals. But on March 20, 1860, after the duo's six long years of gathering petitions, writing letters, making speeches, giving lectures, and offering arguments, New York state finally passed the Married Woman's Property Act. The new law provided married women the right to own their own property, to conduct their own business, and to have joint guardianship of their children, "not subject to control or interference" by their husbands. This law was a large and well-deserved victory.

This 1909 cartoon implied that if women were allowed to vote, men would become housewives.

Election Day!

4
Years of
Struggle

Anthony and Stanton were not just activists for temperance and women's rights. They were also abolitionists who, encouraged by Daniel Anthony and Stanton's husband, Henry, continued speaking out against slavery. While Susan B. Anthony was petitioning for women's property rights, she was offered a job as the New York agent of the American Anti-Slavery Society, an organization headed by the abolitionist leader William Lloyd Garrison. She had turned down the offer at first in order to continue gathering petitions, but two years later, in 1856, she accepted the post.

Her new position paid a small salary and allowed her to use all the skills she had developed as a temperance and women's rights activist. She organized a team of abolitionists and former slaves to give speeches and hang posters, while she set up meetings and arranged schedules. She also made numerous speeches against slavery herself, telling the people of New York, "The guilt rests on the North equally with the South," and, "We ask you to feel as if you, yourselves, were the slaves."

Anthony lost any fears she had about speaking and became a powerful, confident lecturer. However, she had to speak before some tough audiences. Many people, angry and against change, hurled insults and even food at her. In Syracuse, a mob burned a dummy with her name on it. Sometimes she would be allowed to make her presentation, and other times she would have to give up and walk out of the room. Elizabeth Cady Stanton often joined Anthony in these busy halls, as Anthony continued her crusade for women's rights along with the abolition of slavery.

In 1860, shortly after the Married Woman's Property Act was passed, Anthony and Stanton attended the 10th National Woman's Rights Convention. Once again Stanton proposed radical new ideas, such as more liberal divorce laws. She had long thought it important for women to be able to find a legal way out of bad marriages. At the time, women could only run away, often leaving children and property behind.

Anthony and Stanton expected the usual disagreements, because few people wanted to admit that some marriages did not work. They were surprised, however, by their male abolitionist friends, who thus far had supported the women's movement. The men, including William Lloyd Garrison, simply refused to discuss the issue. One angry clergyman told Anthony, "You are not married. You have no business to be discussing marriage." Anthony retorted, "Well, you are not a slave. Suppose you quit lecturing on slavery."

A few months later, Anthony helped a desperate woman and her daughter escape from an abusive husband, who happened to be a state senator. By law the child, who lived in Massachusetts, belonged to the father. Faced with seeing this mother and daughter hurt or separated, Anthony had found them refuge in New York City. When Garrison heard about this, he criticized Anthony. Although he understood why she would undertake such a rescue, he was concerned that her actions could damage his move-

William Lloyd Garrison hired Susan B. Anthony as an antislavery activist but disagreed with some of her more radical demands for women's rights.

ment politically. "Very many abolitionists," Anthony wrote angrily in her diary, "have yet to learn the ABC of women's rights." "Cautious, careful people," she wrote to Stanton, "always casting about to preserve their reputation and social standing, never can bring about a reform."

In 1861, the dispute over slavery, already heated, exploded into civil war. During the painful years that followed, Anthony labored energetically to attract popular support for emancipation (freeing) of the slaves. She and Elizabeth Cady Stanton formed their own antislavery group, called the Woman's National Loyal League. Recalling her earlier success in gathering petitions, Anthony mobilized a new campaign that demanded the absolute abolition of slavery. She approached everyone she knew to collect signatures and raise funds in order to pressure Congress into action.

In 1862, President Abraham Lincoln issued the Emancipation Proclamation, which declared that all slaves in the warring southern states would be set free as of January 1, 1863. Also in 1862, Daniel Anthony died. Grieving over the loss of her father, Susan Anthony vowed to work harder than ever. Stanton, who frequently remained at home to care for her own children, provided emotional support and campaign suggestions to Anthony in long letters. By January 1865, when the Civil War ended, the Woman's National Loyal League had won its fight. It had more than 5,000 members and had collected more than 400,000 signatures for its petition. The Thirteenth Amendment to the Constitution became law, ending slavery.

With the antislavery victory behind her, Susan B. Anthony renewed her crusade for *women's* emancipation. Anthony, though a devoted worker for abolition, had been unhappy with the lull in activity for women's rights during the war. She suggested that the Woman's Rights Association change its name to the Equal Rights Association, and that it focus intensively on a single goal: universal suffrage. Many antislavery supporters were now working for black suffrage, to ensure true citizenship for the people who had recently been freed from bondage. Leaders such as newspaper publisher Horace Greeley, who had previously been supportive, now rejected woman suffrage in their zeal to promote racial equality. "I would sooner cut off my right hand," Anthony countered, "than ask for the ballot for the black man and not for woman."

Congress passed the Fourteenth Amendment in 1866, and it was ratified by the states in 1868, making all people born in the United States legal citizens (but without making any reference to women). The Fifteenth Amendment, proposed and ratified close on its heels, protected citizenship and suffrage for black men. Women, whether white or black, were left out.

Anthony and Stanton had argued against the new amendments because they ignored women. Meanwhile, a friend and fellow feminist, Lucy Stone, was waging a similar campaign in Kansas for joint black and woman suffrage within the state, with similarly disappointing results for women. Stone reported that help was needed if Kansas was to become a model suffrage state. Anthony needed to hear no more.

After visiting her brother Daniel, who lived in Leavenworth, Kansas, she began a new series of lectures, which she gave in barns, sawmills, and wherever else people were willing to assemble. Even with Stanton's help the fight for women's right to vote in Kansas did not succeed. Those desiring suffrage for blacks without suffrage for women spent a great deal of money to oppose the vocal Anthony-Stanton team. Their biggest enemy was the liquor industry, which secretly spent millions of dollars in the campaign against woman suffrage, fearing that women, if they could vote, would make alcohol illegal.

The women did gain a surprising new ally, however. One outspoken man presented the Kansas audiences with a forceful demand for woman suffrage. "Every man in Kansas," he announced, referring to those voting against women's rights, "has insulted his mother, his daughter, his sister, and his wife!" This unusual man was the wealthy and flamboyant George Francis Train. A railroad financier, Train wanted to use his money to help win a woman-suffrage amendment.

Train promised Anthony and Stanton money to publish an equal-rights newspaper. He told them, "Its name is to be the *Revolution*; its motto, 'Men, their rights, and nothing more; women, their rights, and nothing less.'" The two suffragists had long dreamed of publishing such a paper. On January 8, 1868, the first issue of the *Revolution* appeared.

The eccentric Train did not prove a reliable source of financial support, however. After just one issue of the newspaper had appeared, Train went to England, where he was thrown in jail for helping the Irish rebels. For the next three years, Anthony had to raise money to publish the *Revolution* herself.

In 1869, the Equal Rights Association disintegrated. One group, led by Stanton and Anthony, continued to believe women's voting rights were just as important as those of blacks and refused to postpone their own struggle. They formed the National Woman Suffrage Association (NWSA), which sought many other legal rights in addition to suffrage. The other group, including Lucy Stone and Amelia Bloomer, broke off to create the rival American Woman Suffrage Association (AWSA). These women thought it unwise to ask for too much at once, and deferred the fight for women's rights in favor of seeking equality for blacks. They also avoided tackling the thorny issues of equality in marriage, religion, and economic matters.

The AWSA started its own newspaper, the weekly *Women's Journal*. It was edited by men, and its milder opinions made it acceptable to a wider audience. Within a year, it had put the *Revolution* out of business.

Anthony was devastated by this feud with her old friends. For years, she and Stanton had worked with Stone toward similar goals. They were saddened to see friends turn against one

George Francis Train used his wealth to help
Anthony and Stanton start the Revolution, *a newspaper*
that championed women's rights.

another, "instead of fighting the common enemy." But Anthony stated firmly, "The movement cannot be damaged. No 'National' or 'American' . . . can block" its progress.

Lucy Stone, a longtime ally of Anthony's in the fight for woman suffrage, broke with Anthony over her stances on marriage and religion.

The *Revolution* was $10,000 in debt when it was forced to stop publication. Instead of declaring bankruptcy, as most business owners would have done, Anthony vowed to repay every penny that she owed. She embarked immediately on a speechmaking tour to raise money. In 1871 alone she traveled 13,000 miles and gave 171 lectures. It took six grueling years of hard work, but Anthony paid back every cent, winning great praise even from those who disagreed with her.

Susan B. Anthony's 50th birthday party in 1870 was a major event in New York City. Horace Greeley's newspaper, normally critical of Anthony, praised her determination and hard work: "Through these years of disputation and struggling, Miss Anthony has thoroughly impressed friends and enemies alike with the sincerity and earnestness of her purpose." Another paper called her "the Moses of her sex." But as she told her sisters in 1872, the year of her courageous vote, "What I ask is not praise, but justice."

Working together as they had so many times before, Elizabeth Cady Stanton and Susan B. Anthony teamed up in 1881 to write A History of Woman Suffrage.

5

"Failure
Is Impossible"

In 1881, Anthony and Stanton set out to record
their experiences and those of others involved
in the fight for women's rights. Anthony's mother
had died one year earlier, and Anthony was
acutely aware of the progress women had made
during her mother's lifetime. For their book, Anthony and Stanton wrote to every women's rights
activist they knew of. In reply, they received
dozens of personal anecdotes and recollections.

From these stories they created volume one of *A History of Woman Suffrage*. Sadly, one important person's input was missing: Lucy Stone's. Still aloof from the others, Stone had written that she was unable to provide any information. The volume, nevertheless, was a great success. Boosted by a $25,000 inheritance from a wealthy supporter of women's rights, Anthony and Stanton immediately began work on volumes two and three, which were published in 1882 and 1886.

Anthony's inheritance also allowed her and Stanton to take a well-deserved vacation. In England, they met other women who had fought for woman suffrage. Upon her return, Anthony organized an International Council of Women, to be held in Washington, D.C., on the 40th anniversary of the first women's rights convention at Seneca Falls. Stanton, who had remained in England, was not certain that she could return for the convention. Now 73 years old and afraid of the long sea journey home, she told Anthony to proceed without her. Anthony sent Stanton a letter that, she predicted, would "start every white hair on her head." "A fortieth anniversary," Anthony exploded, "of the Seneca Falls convention without the woman who called it!" Two weeks later, Stanton sent a cablegram. "Coming," was all it said, but Anthony understood.

When Stanton arrived just a few days before the council convened she had no speech to present. Anthony put her to work. "Miss Anthony ordered me to remain conscientiously in my own apartment and to prepare a speech," Stanton recalled later. Anthony even placed a guard outside Stanton's door to make sure her partner would complete her task.

Susan B. Anthony opened the first day's session and directed much of the conference, but her happiest moment came when she introduced her lifelong friend. "I have the pleasure of introducing to you this morning," she announced, as she welcomed the council members, "the woman who not only joined with Lucretia Mott in calling the first [women's rights] convention, but who for the greater part of 20 years has been president of the National Woman Suffrage Association—Mrs. Elizabeth Cady Stanton."

The International Council of Women's most significant accomplishment, carried out during the last week in March 1888, was the unification of the many women working for equal rights. Fifty-three organizations from 49 countries had sent representatives to the conference. Even Lucy Stone accepted Anthony's invitation to attend. The members of the National and American Woman Suffrage Associations were now not only willing to begin working together; they even sat next to one another. Susan B. Anthony, Elizabeth Cady Stanton, and Lucy Stone, the "mothers" of the women's movement, looked at one another proudly and recognized what a grand moment the meeting was.

For the first time in 20 years, these women joined hands. In 1890, just two years later, the bond was sealed. Anthony, Stanton, and Stone united their organizations to create the National-American Woman Suffrage Association, and Stanton became its president.

Lucy Stone died in 1891, and Stanton retired the next year. Anthony, as active as ever, took over as president of the suffrage association. In 1893, women won voting rights in Colorado, the second woman suffrage state in the Union after Wyoming (whose female population already had the right to vote when it was admitted as a state in 1890). At the age of 74, Anthony wrote to a friend that she was "traveling from 50 to 100 miles every day and speaking five or six nights a week."

Although Anthony remained healthy, she could not continue to keep the pace she had maintained for 40 years. She believed the time had come for younger women to take over the movement. In 1900, a woman named Carrie Chapman Catt succeeded Anthony, whom newspapers now called "the grand old woman of America." In 1904, Anna Shaw took over for Catt.

The women of Wyoming Territory became the first women in the world to win the right to vote in 1869. When Wyoming was admitted to the Union in 1890, it became the first woman suffrage state.

Anthony continued to guide the younger suffragists, but when Elizabeth Cady Stanton died in 1902, she knew that her time would soon come too. "Mother passed away at three o'clock," Stanton's daughter had telegrammed. A grieving Anthony wrote back, "It seems impossible that voice is stilled which I have loved to hear for 50 years." Left without her lifelong partner in the fight for justice, Anthony was uncertain about what to do next. Stanton had not only been a friend and co-worker, but she had been like a sister and a soul mate. In an effort to ease the pain of her loss, Anthony returned to speechmaking. She attended a meeting of the International Council of Women in Germany, accompanied by her sister Mary, with whom she now lived. In 1906, she attended her last National-American Woman Suffrage Association convention.

Held in Baltimore, Maryland, the annual meeting was as much a celebration of Susan B. Anthony's life and 86th birthday as a meeting on regular suffrage business. "Failure is impossible!"

Twenty thousand suffragists march in New York City in 1915.

she told the huge, cheering crowd at what would be her last public speech.

As she lay ill with pneumonia a month later, she began to recite women's names: important women in her life, other suffragists, fighters for the cause. Elizabeth Cady Stanton, Lucy Stone, Lucretia Mott, Angelina Grimké Weld, Sarah Grimké, Amelia Bloomer, Sojourner Truth . . . "They all seemed to file past her dying eyes that day in an endless shadowy review, and as they went by she spoke to each of them," recalled Anna Shaw, who sat at Anthony's bedside. Susan B. Anthony died in Rochester on March 13, 1906.

Susan B. Anthony, whose dream it was that all women should have the right to vote, died without seeing her dream come true. She had "taken to her soul a purpose," as she once wrote that women must do, and she had worked hard all her life in pursuit of that purpose. There had been many victories. Anthony had proudly noted that the turn of the century found "every trade, voca-

*Shown here in her eighties, Susan B. Anthony
sits surrounded by pictures of other leaders of
the women's rights movement.*

tion, and profession open to women, and every opportunity at their command for preparing themselves to follow these occupations. . . . Woman is no longer compelled to marry for support but may herself make her own home and earn her own financial independence. . . . With but few exceptions, the highest institutions of learning in the land are as freely opened to girls as to boys. . . . There has been a radical revolution in the legal status of women."

But women still could not vote. In 1912, Alice Paul, a young suffragist, organized picketing in front of the White House in Washington, D.C. She vowed, with determination much like Anthony's, that she would protest until women were granted the right to vote.

Seven years later, on May 21, 1919, Congress passed the Nineteenth Amendment to the U.S. Constitution. Ratified by the states in 1920, it became known as the Susan B. Anthony Amendment. It proclaimed, "The rights of citizens of the United States to vote shall not be denied or abridged by the U.S. or any state on account of sex." On the 100th anniversary of Anthony's birth, women had finally won the right to vote.

Further Reading

Other Biographies of Susan B. Anthony

Clinton, Susan. *The Story of Susan B. Anthony.* Chicago: Children's Press, 1986.

Cooper, Ilene. *Susan B. Anthony.* New York: Franklin Watts, 1984.

Monsell, Helen Albee. *Susan B. Anthony: Champion of Women's Rights.* New York: Macmillan, 1986.

Noble, Iris. *Susan B. Anthony.* New York: Messner, 1975.

Peterson, Helen S. *Susan B. Anthony: Pioneer in Women's Rights.* Champaign, IL: Garrard, 1971.

Chronology

Feb. 15, 1820	Born Susan Brownell Anthony in Adams, Massachusetts
1837–1838	Attends the Philadelphia Select Seminary for Females
1840	Works as a teacher at a boarding school in New Rochelle, New York
1845	The Anthony family moves to Rochester, New York
1846–49	Serves as headmistress at Canajoharie Academy
1848	The first women's rights convention is held at Seneca Falls, New York
1849	Anthony makes her first public speech at a women's temperance meeting

1851	Anthony meets Elizabeth Cady Stanton
1852	Anthony organizes the Women's State Temperance Society; Stanton becomes the group's president, Anthony its secretary
1853	Anthony and Stanton leave the Women's State Temperance Union after it is taken over by men and renamed The People's League
1856–64	Serves as the New York State agent for the Anti-Slavery Society
1860	The Married Woman's Property Act is passed; Abraham Lincoln is elected president
1861	The Civil War begins
1863	President Lincoln's Emancipation Proclamation frees blacks living in the South
1868–1870	Anthony and Stanton publish the *Revolution*
1869	Anthony and Stanton found the National Woman Suffrage Association; Lucy

Stone forms the American Woman Suffrage Association

1872 Anthony is arrested for voting illegally

1881 Anthony and Stanton publish *A History of Woman Suffrage*

1888 Anthony forms the International Council of Women; the National Woman Suffrage Association and the American Woman Suffrage Association join forces

1890 Wyoming is granted statehood, becoming the first state in which women have the right to vote

Mar. 13, 1906 Susan B. Anthony dies of pneumonia in Rochester, New York

Aug. 26, 1920 The Nineteenth Amendment is adopted, giving women the right to vote

Glossary

abolitionist one who believed that slavery should be abolished, or ended

ballot the sheet of paper used to cast a vote in secrecy; also, the act of voting

bloomers the pantaloon costume, named after Amelia Bloomer, that became popular during the 1850s among suffragists

Emancipation Proclamation the declaration issued by President Abraham Lincoln in which he proclaimed that as of January 1, 1863, all slaves in the southern states were free

Fifteenth Amendment the addition to the U.S. Constitution, adopted in 1870, that forbids a state to deny a person the right to vote because of race, color, or previous condition of servitude

Fourteenth Amendment the addition to the U.S. Constitution, adopted in 1868, that defines U.S. citizenship and prohibits states from denying any person life, liberty, and property without due process of law

Nineteenth Amendment the addition to the U.S. Constitution, adopted in 1920, also known as the Susan B. Anthony Amendment, which prohibits any state from denying the right to vote to any citizen because of sex

Quaker A member of the Society of Friends, a religious group that believes that no priest or ritual is needed to communicate with God; Quakers believe in the equality of men and women, and they oppose violence

ratify to approve formally by law

rights powers or privileges

suffrage the right to vote

suffragist one who supports the right of women to vote

temperance movement the movement to restrict or forbid the sale and use of alcoholic beverages

Thirteenth Amendment the addition to the U.S. Constitution, adopted in 1865, forbidding slavery in the United States

U.S. Constitution   the document that defines the basic laws of the United States and the duties of the government and guarantees certain rights to the people

women's rights movement   the collective struggle to end the domination of women by men and to gain equal rights between the sexes

Index

Pamela Levin is a writer and artist living in Milan, Italy. She earned a B.A. in humanities at the New College in Sarasota, Florida, and formerly worked as a copywriter at Yale University Press.